MW01631424

# RUMI

## Words of Wisdom

101 Quotations Curated and Compiled to Instantly Expand Your Mind and Experience Consciousness

Curated and Compiled by

**Maitreyi Gautam**

**INSPIRING WORDS PICTURE BOOK SERIES**

Published by FastRead Books

First Edition

**Copyright**

Copyright 2018. All rights reserved.

This curated and compiled work is copyrighted as derivative work. The quotations and certain images are available in the public domain. No part of this publication may be reproduced, distributed or transmitted in any form or by any means, including photocopying, recording or other electronic or mechanical methods, without the prior written permission of the publisher, except in case of brief quotation embodied in critical reviews and certain other noncommercial uses permitted by Copyright law. For permission request, write to the Copyright holder using contact form at Publisher website www.FastRead.ca, addressed "Attention: Permissions Coordinator".

**Disclaimer and Consumer Notice**

The compiler **and publisher cannot guarantee the accuracy of any of the information mentioned herein.** Please check with your local authorities regarding any limitations with regards to any concepts presented in this book.

ISBN: 978-1-988969-09-1

## A Brief Introduction to Rumi

Jalal ad-Din Muhammad Rumi was a 13th. century Persian poet, theologian and a Sufi mystic. Rumi's works are written mostly in Persian, though occasionally he also used Turkish, Arabic, and Greek words. Rumi was originally from the Balkh, in present-day Afghanistan. When the Mongols invaded Central Asia, Rumi along with his family and a group of disciples, set out westwards.

It is believed that during his migration to Persia (modern day Iran), Rumi encountered one of the most famous and mystic Persian poets, Attar, who recognized Rumi's spiritual eminence. It is then that Attar gave the young Rumi his Asrārnāma, a book about the entanglement of the soul in the material world. This meeting had a deep impact on the eighteen-year-old Rumi and later became the inspiration for his works.

A few years later, when Rumi met the dervish Shams-e Tabrizi; it completely transformed his life. From an accomplished teacher and jurist, Rumi became an ascetic.

Rumi died on December 17, 1273 in Konya. His body was interred beside that of his father and a splendid shrine was erected over his place of burial. The profound wisdom of Rumi's teachings is clearly indicated by his epitaph, which reads: "When we are dead, seek not our tomb in the earth, but find it in the hearts of men."

The influence of Rumi's work transcends borders, religions and beliefs! Each of the following quotation is not merely a statement, but 'jewels of wisdom'. They convey Rumi's understanding of the innate workings of life, nature and our very existence.

Rumi's words have the profound ability to expand our mind and senses, so we can gain insightful understanding of our true essential nature of existence; our conscious reality and beyond.

- Maitreyi Gautam

*Your task is not to seek for love, but merely to seek and find all the barriers within yourself that you have built against it.*

*You are not a drop in the ocean.*
*You are the entire ocean, in a drop.*

*Let silence take you to the core of life.*

*Yesterday I was clever, so I wanted to change the world. Today I am wise, so I am changing myself.*

*Everyone has been made for some particular work, and the desire for that work has been put in every heart.*

*The desire to know your own soul will end all other desires.*

*You are not meant for crawling, so don't. You have wings. Learn to use them and fly.*

*Let yourself become living poetry.*

*Be drunk with love, for love is all that exists.*

*Be soulful. Be kind. Be in love.*

*Be an empty page, untouched by words.*

*Maybe you are searching among the branches, for what only appears in the roots.*

*There is a voice that doesn't use words, listen.*

*In silence there is eloquence. Stop weaving and see how the pattern improves.*

*I am not this hair, I am not this skin, I am the soul that lives within.*

*These pains you feel are messengers. Listen to them.*

*When the world pushes you to your knees, you're in the perfect position to pray.*

*Be full of sorrow, that you may become hill of joy; weep, that you may break into laughter.*

*Stop acting so small. You are the universe in ecstatic motion.*

*It's your road and yours alone. Others may walk it with you, but no one can walk it for you.*

*Let silence be the art you practice.*

*Wisdom tells us we are not worthy; love tells us we are. My life flows between the two.*

*I have been a seeker and I still am, but I stopped asking the books and the stars. I started listening to the teaching of my Soul.*

*In the blackest of your moments,
wait with no fear.*

*I want to sing like the birds sing, not worrying about who hears or what they think.*

*The whole universe is contained within a single human being - you.*

*Seek the sound that never ceases.*
*Seek the sun that never sets.*

*Conventional opinion is the ruin of our souls.*

*Whatever purifies you is the right path, I will not try to define it.*

*Let go of your mind and then be mindful. Close your ears and listen.*

*Grief can be the garden of compassion. If you keep your heart open through everything, your pain can become your greatest ally in your life's search for love and wisdom.*

*The wound is the place where the light enters you.*

*But listen to me. For one moment quit being sad. Hear blessings dropping their blossoms around you.*

*Wherever you are, and whatever you do, be in love.*

*Close your eyes, fall in love, stay there.*

*Love is the bridge between you and everything.*

*We carry inside us the wonders we seek outside us.*

*Your heart knows the way. Run in that direction.*

*What you seek is seeking you.*

*Let the beauty we love be what we do.*

*Let yourself be silently drawn by the stronger pull of what you really love.*

*Concentrate on the Essence,*
*Concentrate on the light.*

*Why do you stay in prison when the door is so wide open?*

*Beyond the rightness or wrongness of things there is a field, I'll meet you there.*

*Raise your words, not voice. It is rain that grows flowers, not thunder.*

*When you do things from your soul, you feel a river moving in you, a joy.*

*Life is balance of holding on and letting go.*

*Patience is the key to joy.*

*If light is in your heart, you will find your way home.*

*Set your life on fire. Seek those who fan your flames.*

*Whenever they rebuild an old building, they must first of all destroy the old one.*

*Your radiance shines in every atom of creation yet our petty desires keep it hidden.*

*Everything about yesterday has gone with yesterday. Today, it is needed to say new things.*

*The world is a mountain, in which your words are echoed back to you.*

*The moment you accept what troubles you've been given, the door will open.*

*When you lose all sense of self, the bonds of a thousand chains will vanish.*

*Peaceful is the one who's not concerned with having more or less. Unbound by name and fame, he is free from sorrow from the world and mostly from himself.*

*Everything is emptiness. Everything else, accidental. Emptiness brings peace to your loving.*

*In their seeking, wisdom and madness are one and the same. On the path of love, friend and stranger are one and the same.*

*Inside any deep asking is the answering.*

*The illuminated life can happen now, in the moments left. Die to your ego, and become a true human being.*

*If you are irritated by every rub,*
*how will your mirror be polished?*

*Everything else, disease. In this world of trickery, emptiness is what your soul wants.*

*Anything which is more than our necessity is Poison. It may be power, wealth, hunger, ego, greed, laziness, love, ambition, hate or anything.*

*As you start to walk on the way,*
*the way appears.*

*When you seek love with all your heart you shall find its echo in the universe.*

*One of the marvels of the world:*
*The sight of a soul sitting in*
*prison with the key in its hand.*

*If you love someone, you are always joined with them - in joy, in absence, in solitude, in strife.*

*On the path of love we are neither masters nor the owners of our lives. We are only a brush in the hand of the master painter.*

*Everyone is overridden by thoughts; that's why they have so much heartache and sorrow.*

*Friendship of the wise is good; a wise enemy is better than a foolish friend.*

*Be grateful for your life, every detail of it, and your face will come to shine like a sun, and everyone who sees it will be made glad and peaceful.*

*Why struggle to open a door between us when the whole wall is an illusion?*

*Our greatest strength lies in the gentleness and tenderness of our heart.*

*Your heart is the size of an ocean. Go find yourself in its hidden depths.*

*Let the waters settle and you will see the moon and the stars mirrored in your own being.*

*Wherever water flows, life flourishes: wherever tears fall, divine mercy is shown.*

*Every need brings what's needed.*
*Pain bears its cure like a child.*
*Having nothing produces provisions.*
*Ask a difficult question, and the*
*marvelous answer appears.*

*The soul has been given its own ears to hear things mind does not understand.*

*The message behind the words is the voice of the heart.*

*I learned that every mortal will taste death. But only some will taste life.*

*Come out of the circle of time and into the circle of love.*

*What hurts you, blesses you.*
*Darkness is your candle.*

*We came whirling out of nothingness, scattering stars like dust... The stars made a circle, and in the middle, we dance.*

*Do not feel lonely, the entire universe is inside you.*

*In order to understand the dance one must be still. And in order to truly understand stillness one must dance.*

*Knock, and He'll open the door. Vanish, and He'll make you shine like the sun. Fall, and He'll raise you to the heavens. Become nothing, and He'll turn you into everything.*

*The breeze at dawn has secrets to tell you. Don't go back to sleep.*

*Make peace with the universe. Take joy in it. It will turn to gold. Resurrection will be now. Every moment, a new beauty.*

*Don't you know yet? It is your Light that lights the worlds.*

*Truth lifts the heart, like water refreshes thirst.*

*How do I know who I am or where I am? How could a single wave locate itself in an ocean.*

*Silence is the language of God,*
*all else is poor translation.*

*Ways of worshipping are not to be ranked as better or worse than one another... It's all praise, and it's all right.*

*Now be silent. Let the One who creates the words speak. He made the door. He made the lock. He also made the key.*

*Put your thoughts to sleep, do not let them cast a shadow over the moon of your heart. Let go of thinking.*

*The beauty you see in me is a reflection of you.*

*We rarely hear the inward music, but we're all dancing to it nevertheless.*

*I searched for God and found only myself. I searched for myself and found only God.*

*Goodbyes are only for those who love with their eyes. Because for those who love with heart and soul there is no such thing as separation.*

*There is a loneliness more precious than life. There is a freedom more precious than the world. Infinitely more precious than life and the world is that moment when one is alone with God.*

# Bringing it all together

This is not a book which we can simply read through and put down. Each of these quotations are meant to be read, re-read and mulled over to understand their true meaning.

As you contemplate each quotation and meditate on its deeper meaning, you will start gaining new insights into the innate wisdom conveyed by these seemingly simple words. Each iteration of contemplation will bring you added nuances of understanding.

I hope you find immense benefit from these profound quotations by a wise ascetic, poet and above all a true seeker- Rumi.

\- Maitreyi Gautam

# Review

As we prepare to close, I must ask you for a favor. Great reviews mean everything in publishing. If this book helps or inspires you in any way, please take a moment to leave this work a positive review and share it with your friends and family.

Thanks a million…

*- Maitreyi Gautam*

Maitreyi Gautam comes from the original Vedic Tradition. In Maitreyi Paradigm, she brings various insights, lessons and at times modern-interpretations of ancient techniques and methods. She tries to bring the wisdom of ancient, insightful ways to benefit a modern, evolving and conscious lifestyle.

Think of her work as "Spirituality for the Rest-of-Us". It is for people who have families, careers, material goals & ambitions. The information on Maitreyi Paradigm website is for people who cannot simply extrapolate what typical spiritual gurus and guides say while living special monastic lives. She brings practical "walking the path" wisdom to Conscious Living.

You can read more about her work and contact her at:

**www.MaitreyiParadigm.com**

# Thank you for your purchase

We thank you very much for reading this book and hope you will also enjoy other books by FastRead.

Please feel free to let us know your feedback. It will help us to improve future editions.

Best Regards,

**Editor in Chief**

**FastRead Books, Canada**

Website: www.FastRead.ca

# Other books by Maitreyi Gautam

# Other publications by FastRead Books

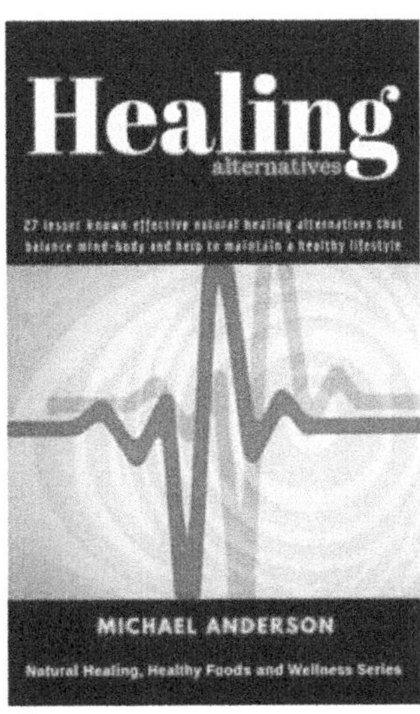

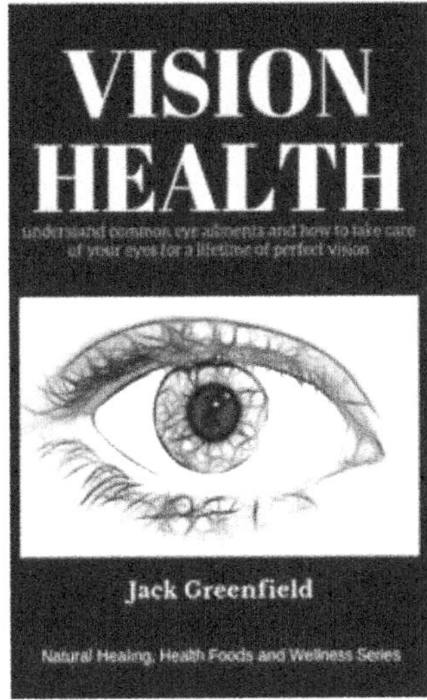

… and there are many more titles.

Please check out all our book titles at:

www.FastRead.ca

Made in the USA
Monee, IL
03 June 2020